FROM WORKPLACE TO WORKSPACE

Using Email Lists to Work Together

Maureen James & Liz Rykert

INTERNATIONAL DEVELOPMENT RESEARCH CENTRE

Ottawa • Cairo • Johannesburg • Montevideo • Nairobi • New Delhi • Singapore

Published by the International Development Research
Centre
PO Box 8500, Ottawa, ON, Canada K1G 3H9

January 1998

Legal deposit: 1st quarter 1998
National Library of Canada
ISBN 0-88936-848-1

The catalogue of IDRC Books may be consulted online at
http://www.idrc.ca/index_e.html

iii

CONTENTS

Part I: Getting Set Up

Part II: Working Together

iv

Part III: Resources

FOREWORD

Next to the telephone and fax machine, electronic mail —
or email — is the most pervasive communication tool in
existence today. Although innovative information and
communication technologies (ICTs) are emerging daily, the
lack of reliable and speedy access to these tools limits their
usefulness for people in nonindustrialized countries. Access
to email currently extends much further into these regions
of the world than does any other Internet-based technology.
Consequently, electronic mailing lists have evolved as a
powerful tool for collaboration. Many people, however,
have no experience in using an electronic mailing list to
work together. It can be a frustrating and sometimes
intimidating experience.

The idea for this guide arose as a result of an informal
discussion on mailing lists between the Unganisha project of
Canada's International Development Research Centre
(IDRC) and the Bellanet International Secretariat. There was
unanimous recognition of the need to promote the use of
mailing lists and of the dearth of concise and helpful
documentation on their use. Through this guide, IDRC and
Bellanet hope to address both of these issues.

IDRC's Unganisha project was initiated in early 1997 with a
mandate to assist IDRC-funded researchers in gaining
access to email and the Internet. Its mission is to assist
researchers in sharing research information and
collaborating on projects.

The Bellanet International Secretariat, established by a
group of donor organizations, works to improve the impact
and relevance of development program planning and
cooperation through the use of ICTs. The cornerstones of

Bellanet's program are stakeholder participation, transparency, knowledge diffusion, and collaboration.

We hope that you find this guide useful in your online work. Please send your comments to guide@unganisha.idrc.ca.

Steve Song
International Development
   Research Centre
ssong@idrc.ca
http://www.idrc.ca/unganisha

Riff Fullan
Bellanet International
Secretariat
riff@bellanet.org
http://www.bellanet.org

WELCOME TO THIS GUIDE!

Electronic mailing lists are a cost-effective way to bring people with common interests together. Working together online allows your group to:

✓ save money on long-distance phone calls, conference calls, faxing, and travel

✓ easily share documents, information and relevant resources

✓ involve more people than face-to-face meetings allow

✓ keep an ongoing centrally accessible archive of your group's work

✓ involve people when it's convenient for them

✓ have a place to collaborate between face-to-face meetings

✓ build and strengthen your community of interest.

This guide will help you decide how to set up a mailing list for your group, launch it and keep it active.

Mailing lists can serve all sorts of collaborative functions: some are used for short-term, concentrated action planning across a closed group; others are available for ongoing general information sharing and discussion on a particular topic. No matter how public or private, immediate or long-term, successful mailing lists have four critical requirements: a committed group of participants, a shared purpose, good facilitation and a well-organized plan.

The information in this guide is organized according to the stages a facilitator goes through in preparing to use a mailing list to work productively with a group of people. We've divided it into three parts:

Getting Set Up

- Provides an overview of mailing lists and how to prepare your group to use them.

- Finishes with a checklist to be used as a quick reference guide to keep you on track throughout.

Working Together

- Introduces the concepts of online facilitation and how to apply them to your group's work.

- Outlines how lists can be used for specific group activities.

Resources

- Answers typical real-life questions that arise when facilitating mailing lists.

- Provides references to further reading and online resources.

When you're done with this guide, you should be well on your way to designing a list that will meet the unique needs of your group.

Part I

GETTING SET UP

OVERVIEW

What Mailing Lists Are and How They Work

Email is the simplest and most readily available form of online communication. Because email concepts correspond closely to regular postal mail, even people who have never used the Internet before can learn email fundamentals and quickly become comfortable. From there, it's not too daunting to be part of a group working together using a mailing list.

Mailing lists allow any number of people with email addresses to communicate amongst one another on issues of common interest. A mailing list is an automatic message-sending program that stores a list of the email addresses of all the people interested in a particular discussion. Participants "subscribe" to the list. If they decide they no longer want to receive messages from the list, they can "unsubscribe". Each discussion has its own email address (e.g., devel-l@american.edu). Each time a message is posted to the list address, everyone subscribed to the mailing list receives it.

How People Are Using Them

Groups can do just about everything they do face-to-face using a mailing list, and often more. Here are just a few examples:

- a number of independent community economic development officers in South America and Eastern Africa are linked to each other to share strategies and develop policy documents together

- a rainforest sustainability program officer from a donor agency keeps in touch with local officers and researchers at several rainforest field stations

- in advance of a continental meeting on development and gender, concerned individuals and experts from around the world discuss key issues and collaborate on proposals to be presented at the face-to-face conference

- a board of directors carries on between-meeting discussions and develops the next meeting agenda

- a fundraising working group for an international environmental research organization shares leads, tactics and develops funding proposals together.

Why Choose a Mailing List?

There are many different types of online group collaboration tools: basic email, WWW-based conferencing systems, newsgroups, Internet Relay Chat (IRC), video and audio-conferencing, and Intranets, for example. Your group may want to explore some of these other methods if they are readily available to all of you. Regardless of the tool you choose, you'll need to facilitate your group's use of it. This guide focuses on mailing lists because they are an inexpensive, universal collaboration tool that anyone with an email account anywhere in the world can use.

What You Need to Get Started

Successful mailing lists share these elements:

✓ a common purpose among participants

✓ a group that is committed to using email regularly for working together

✓ a facilitator to pull everything together and keep it moving

✓ a plan for how the list should work

You'll also need to find an Internet Service Provider that offers a mailing list service — most do!

There are different types of mailing list software, the most commonly used being: Majordomo, ListProc and Listserv. Which you have access to depends on your Internet service provider. (An *Internet Service Provider* is the computer network you connect to where your email account resides.) From a user/subscriber perspective, these different programs all perform similar subscription and message management functions, but each has unique commands and tools for doing so.

PLANNING YOUR LIST

Collaboration and information exchange doesn't automatically happen when a mailing list is set up. Mailing lists require preparation and planning to make them useful, and a group committed to working together online. Before launching it, you should put together a plan for your list, based on the answers to these questions:

? Who will use the list?

? What will it be used for?

? How ready is your group?

Who Will Use the List?

You can control who has access to your mailing list. It can be open to anyone interested in a particular topic, or closed to a specific group of people. Another possibility is to limit active participation to a particular group of people, but make the discussion available on a read-only basis to anyone on the Internet. How you set your list up depends on what you plan to use it for.

Here are some questions for you to consider:

? What is the purpose of the list: is it for general information-sharing (in which case the group may be more open) or to collaborate on a particular project or campaign (which may narrow the field of participants)?

? Are there others beyond the immediate group members who will benefit from seeing the work of your group as you do it?

? How important are privacy considerations to the work being done?

? Is yours a tightly-knit group working closely on a particular project that prefers a workers-only roll-up-your-sleeves space so you can feel free to say what you want? Or can it be open to others less directly involved in the project — advisors, board members, volunteers, funders, and others?

Here are some examples:

- A mailing list that links people in different countries working on projects related to indigenous crop preservation is used primarily for sharing information, resources, experiences and news among practitioners. Active participation on the list is open only to practitioners, however the discussion is copied to a public read-only site on the Internet for anyone interested to monitor.

- The discussion on a private mailing list that links organizations working to end female genital mutilation, due to the controversial subject matter, is available only to those people who are approved to participate.

- A short-term list set up to develop and implement a working group's presentation at a face-to-face conference is open only to those making the presentation, and the list is discontinued once the presentation has been made.

List access privileges can be expanded, contracted or changed as the need arises. If you choose to set up a closed list, you'll need to establish a decision-making process for admitting or removing participants. Be sure everyone knows who has access to the list when it is launched, and inform your group before any changes take place. People are more comfortable posting messages when they know who is receiving them.

What Will You Use Your List For?

Before you start to use your list, it's essential to have a plan of action for how it will be used. Think about the individuals you plan to bring together electronically, and assess the ways you work together now. Ideally, your mailing list should enhance your face-to-face and voice-to-voice communication.

Here are some questions to work through with your group to help build your mailing list strategy. Your group's answers to these questions will become more clear as you work through the rest of this guide. We've also provided sample list plans below.

Current Communication Patterns

? How often does this group communicate at face-to-face meetings, or by phone, fax and postal mail?

? For what purpose(s) is this group currently communicating?

? Who currently initiates communication among the whole group?

? Who else should be included on the mailing list now that travel expense and time zones are no longer barriers?

Group Characteristics

? Are decisions made within this group? How? Can this be done online?

? What is the work pace of the group?

? Is every member of the group committed to working online and able to do so?

? How often will each person check email?

Information Sharing

? Who assembles information for the group? Is this a task the group could share responsibility for?

? What types of information resources does this group generate? How will these be made available to list members?

Online Work Planning

? What are some specific outcomes to be working towards on the list?

? What are some focused online activities that would be useful to the group? e.g., regular updates from each community or program area; joint preparation of reports or funding proposals; sharing research findings; planning and holding meetings, etc.

8

? Does part or all of this group relate to other initiatives? Are these other networks communicating online? How can links be made with other relevant online work?

To give you a better idea of what a group ends up with after dealing with these questions, here are two sample list plans — one for a group that is already working together offline, and one for a group that has similar interests but hasn't actually coalesced into a working group.

GROUP 1:
Already Working Together Offline

The executive committee of a pan-american women's health organization consists of 7 members, based in 2 continents and 7 countries. Currently, this group gets together face-to-face 3 times per year for 2-3 days, arranged where possible in conjunction with other events that most or all of the members are attending. Meeting agendas and regional reports are faxed to members a week in advance of the face-to-face meetings. Conference calls for program updates and any other current issues take place once per month on the 3rd Tuesday in the evening. Between-call urgent issues are dealt with by the Chair in consultation with at least one other executive committee member, and reported on at the monthly conference call. To save money and to increase convenience, the group has decided to use a mailing list for their regular communication. Here's the draft plan:

For the first year, the secretary of the executive committee will be the facilitator of the mailing list. The group has decided to meet only once per year face-to-face, and to plan and hold the rest of their meetings and conference calls on the mailing list. Each member is responsible for a different aspect of the organization's programming, and will post a monthly update. Regional reports will be posted by the members themselves. Each member is expected to check in at least once per week. There are 2 in the group who aren't yet fully online, but who have committed to getting connected and trained within 3 months. During that time, the secretary will continue to keep in touch with them by phone and fax, and be their liaison to the mailing list, as well as provide support getting them hooked up.

Due to the sensitive nature of some of their discussions, the executive committee has decided not to make their mailing list open to the larger 25-member board of directors (many of whom are not online yet), but will regularly circulate updates and meeting minutes to those with email addresses.

The executive committee has an already established consensus-based decision-making mechanism. Where consensus cannot be reached, a ⅔ majority vote carries the decision. When an issue is put to a vote, the group has established that silence means acceptance.

The group has committed to a "learn together by doing" approach and the facilitator will engage the group in discussions of any problems regarding list use as they arise. The committee will review the effectiveness of the list at an online meeting 6 months after the list is launched, and will decide then whether modifications need to be made.

GROUP 2:
Not Already Working
Together Offline

A program officer at a funding agency is aware that there are several funded projects related to medicinal plants research going on in different parts of the world that would benefit from closer collaboration. Many of the researchers often see each other at conferences and meetings and communicate with each other sporadically, but don't actually have a group working relationship. The program officer, who has taken on the facilitation role, contacts the individuals to see if they are interested in collaborating online — where they will have the opportunity to build on each other's work, share resources and contacts, as well as lessons learned, and perhaps develop joint initiatives.

In this case, the group needs to spend more time working out the reasons for coming together in the first place, and then defining mechanisms for using the list to accomplish these tasks. For example, if the researchers prioritize sharing information, then each could take responsibility for reporting on a particular issue area, in addition to posting their own work.

The role of the facilitator in this situation is more complex: not only are you establishing a mailing list, but your group will also be coming to terms with working together as a new group. You will likely not be able to answer as many of the planning questions as a group that already has established working relationships. You may need to put in more effort at the beginning as many participants may see the mailing list as "more work" on top of their regular work, until the group begins to get tangible results from the collaboration. You should expect the use of the list to change and evolve as the group members get to know one another and begin collaborating.

Working through these planning questions will help you develop a strategy for your group's mailing list. It will also help you build an online workspace that enhances the strengths and means of your group's current communication methods. You can shape the mailing list, your primary communications tool, to fit the work the group needs to do together. Bear in mind that your plan and what actually happens on the list may be different, but going through the process of answering the questions will prepare you well for working together online.

How Ready is Your Group?

You need to make sure that people will be able to use your list once it is set up. Some in your group may be brand new users, others may be accustomed to high-tech tools. Still others may not have used email before. During the planning phase, check with each person to gauge how ready and willing they are to participate. Here are the key things to find out:

Equipment

Each participant must have regular access to an email account that connects to the Internet. Your group may be spread out across the country or around the world, and it's likely that each person will have a unique way of connecting. You may need to help some people find out how to connect to your list from where they're based.

Keep in mind that not everyone will be using the same equipment or software. Some may be using IBM-compatibles, and some may be using Macintoshes, for example, and they may all be running different operating systems. Not everyone will be using the latest technology — some may be using text-only communications software. If people contact you for help, the problems they describe may be completely different from your experience. Watch for those who share common ways of connecting. People using similar systems are in a good position to support each other. This helps to distribute responsibility for support and build group cohesion and sustainability.

Access

Your group will likely encounter varying levels of access to the Internet within their own countries. For example, not all computer networks in Africa offer direct Internet access. Some make a connection to a nearby network that does have direct access. Also, phone connections in many places are unreliable, so there may be delays of several days or sometimes weeks before a person can post messages. It's good to know who is in this situation, as you will need to leave a longer amount of time for them to respond to issues where their input is needed. Sometimes you may need to use alternative communication means as a backup, such as phone or fax, to enable the participation of those with unreliable connections.

There may be some in your group that don't have email accounts. You can do some research to point them to local access providers, and help get them set up. Of those who already have email accounts, find out how regularly they use them and if they are comfortable doing so. Those who aren't will need extra support at the beginning, and you should build this into your planning.

Enthusiasm

In every group of people making the move to online collaboration, there are always some people who are really excited about the opportunity, some who are willing to suspend their disbelief and give it a try, and others who energetically resist. Some may never want to know more than the basics of getting connected to the list. As a facilitator it's your job to offer extra encouragement and be available to those who need it.

Experience

People working together online is a relatively new development. Many will have used the Internet primarily for sending and receiving email, and for browsing WWW sites, but never have tried to use it for working collaboratively. Keep in mind that you are breaking new ground as your group begins to coalesce on the mailing list. Each participant will have unique skills, experiences and habits to bring to your list. The more you learn about each other in the beginning, the easier it will be to get everyone working together.

SETTING UP YOUR LIST

Once you've planned a strategy with your group, here's how to set your list up.

Definitions

The "listowner" is the person technically administrating the list who receives automatically generated email messages from the list software. (This is not necessarily the same person as the facilitator, and you can choose to have multiple listowners.)

A "list subscriber" is someone who has signed up to participate on the list.

The "list server" is the computer that operates the mailing lists carried by the service provider.

Which Software?

Find out from your service provider which mailing list software they offer. ListProc, Majordomo, and Listserv are the three most commonly used. It's likely that your service provider will only run one type. They all perform basically the same functions, but in different ways. Service providers usually charge a one-time setup fee to create mailing lists.

Mailing List Settings

Tell your service provider that you want to set up a mailing list. They will probably give you a mailing list setup form to fill out. Mailing lists come with a lot of customizable options that you can set to meet your group's unique needs. Which you choose will depend on what your group intends to do together online, and whether it's an open or closed group. Consult with the group when making these decisions. These settings can always be changed after your mailing list has been set up, however you should check first if the service provider charges to make changes.

An overview of some of the important settings and their implications are presented here.

Name: Choose an easily recognizable, brief name for your list. Some lists are named for the organization sponsoring the list, e.g., ACACIA-L: A discussion forum operated by IDRC's ACACIA program for issues relating to information technology and development in Africa. Others refer to what the list is about: e.g., DEVEL-L is a list to discuss technology transfer in international development.

Listowner: Give the email address of at least one person who will "own" or technically administrate the list. Listowner responsibilities include: subscribing and unsubscribing people (on a closed list), dealing with "bounces" (messages that don't make it to the list for various reasons) and other list administration work. The amount of work depends on how active your list is and how familiar your group is with mailing lists. It can also depend on system conditions at your Internet service provider. If they are having technical problems, the listowner workload may increase proportionately.

The listowner is given a password to do this work. You can specify more than one listowner, which is often a good idea, especially for a large list. Continuously administrating a list can create a sense of undue pressure on anyone doing the work single-handedly. You may want to go on vacation or need to be away from time to time and having more than one person in the listowner role means the work can be divided to ensure coverage and continuity.

Digest: Some subscribers prefer to receive the list messages in one summary message rather than individually as they get posted to the list. The summary message is called a "digest". Digest setup options vary. For example, with ListProc, it's up to the user to send a command to the list requesting the digest version. With Majordomo, you set up a separate list for the digest version. You can also set the size of the digest message. We recommend 40K or lower because some service providers don't allow incoming messages over this size. The message content of both the regular version and the digest version of the list is exactly the same, it's just the timing of message delivery that's different. A disadvantage of digests is that all the messages are contained in one, making it harder to sort and respond to individual postings.

Restricted Access: When your mailing list is set up as "restricted", each subscriber has to be "approved" by the listowner before being allowed in. Across the Internet, there have been increasing problems with non-restricted lists being "attacked" (also known as "spammed") by pranksters who flood the list with irrelevant or disturbing postings. As a result, many service providers no longer allow you to set up non-restricted lists. Even if they do offer non-restricted lists, we recommend you set yours up as restricted. Restricted lists mean more work for the listowner ("approving" each new subscriber), but your list will be protected from outside troublemakers.

If your list is set up for a closed group, you'll know in advance who should have access, and will approve only those subscribers, and ignore any others who try to gain access. If it's a public one, it's rare that you'll know who all of the subscribers are so approving them is more of a rubber-stamp process. The advantage of a restricted list is that the listowner can unsubscribe someone who refuses to follow the ground rules established by list members.

Moderated vs. Unmoderated: One way to manage the activity on your list is to "approve" each message before it gets posted. This is a lot of work for the listowner, particularly on an active list. This has been used as a way of controlling the types of postings that make it onto the list. One example where moderation is used is for a "news bulletin" type of list, where you need to make sure that every posting is from an authorized source. As long as your group is clear about the purpose of the list and how it will function, and if it's already "restricted" (see above), we recommend that you not set the list to be moderated. Start unmoderated, and only if you find a need to keep strict control of what gets posted would you consider moderating the list.

Advertised: If yours is a public list, you can set it up so that the name and a short description appear in a public "list of lists" that everyone on the Internet has access to. If it's a private list, you probably won't want to do this, so you would choose that advertising be turned "off".

Your "info" File: Every mailing list has an "information" file included with it. Each new subscriber receives a message with this "information" in it when they subscribe. This is an important introductory document where you outline the purpose of your list as well as any other information that is pertinent to your subscribers: how the list will function, basic instructions for using the list, what the settings are (for example, if it is moderated people should know), how you expect the group to work together, how to find and use the archives, etc. You can make changes to your info file as your list evolves. It's a good idea to check it once a month or so, to see that it's still relevant.

Remember that mailing list participants see messages as they get posted. If they subscribe after the list has started, they will have missed the initial postings. Make sure your info file addresses everything a newcomer would need to know, so that they can catch up quickly. Also, if you have set up archiving (see below), make reference to where the archive is located and how to use it so that new subscribers can see what has transpired.

Here is a sample "info" file:

(Note: Addresses in this sample are fictitious.)

```
Welcome to the gender-dev mailing list!

To catch up on what's been going on...
Archives of this mailing list are available at:

http://www.idrc.ca/archives/gender-dev/

If you don't have WWW access, you can send an email
message with no subject to:

getweb@idrc.ca
with the following text:
get http://www.idrc.ca/archives/genderdev/

The purpose of this discussion is to share information
and resources among people working on gender and
development issues, particularly as they relate to
technological development.

Be sure to sign in and tell us about yourself, your work,
your interests and experiences!

::: To Post Messages

To post a new message to the discussion, address it to:

        gender-dev@listproc.idrc.ca

If you are responding to someone else's posting, please
make sure the Subject heading is the same as the one
you're replying to, so discussion stays relatively
coherent.

::: Collaborating Effectively
```

To keep this a productive workspace, we ask you to
observe three rules:
1. Messages must be relevant to gender, development and
technology.
2. Please treat each other with respect.
3. When you would like to have a personal discussion, or
if you feel offended by a particular message, please send
a message to the individual involved only.

::: General Usage Guidelines

o Please introduce yourself in your first posting.
o Try to keep postings concise and short, ideally two
screens worth or less.

o Please do *not* keep the body of the original text in
your replies, except as absolutely necessary. Access and
downloading charges are particularly expensive in the
South.

o Use a descriptive Subject header to identify message
content. That way, people can more easily decide which
messages they want to read. When you respond to a message,
keep the original subject heading intact unless it is no
longer relevant to your message content.

::: Text-Only Access
Many of the people participating in this discussion do
not have full Internet access. To ensure equitable access
to the discussion and information, we ask you to do the
following:

o If you are referencing resources that are available via
WWW, please also let us know how we can receive them via
email, so that those without WWW access can access them.

o For accented text (i.e., non-English messages), please
strip the accents and replace them with unaccented
letters, e.g., espanol francais etc.

If you have questions, concerns or suggestions about the
operation of this list, please direct them to the list
facilitator: sthomas@idrc.ca

Password: Each mailing list is set up with a password
that only the listowners know, to ensure that they are
the only ones able to make changes to the list settings.
Choose one with a combination of upper and lower case
letters, and numbers. For example, your list password
might be: Dm7vYa

Reply-To: You have a choice of having reply messages
go directly to the list address, or to the person who
posted the message being responded to. Most often, lists
are set up so that replies go to the list directly. This
ensures continuity and transparency of discussion.

Changes to List Settings: Let your group know if you are planning to change the settings on the list. If for example, you switch your list from being a public one to a private one, or from moderated to unmoderated, you'll need to give advance warning to the people already using it, and explain why you are altering the settings. It's important to check with the group before making these types of decisions, so that they don't come as a surprise. Often, the impetus for these changes comes from the group itself, in response to things that happen on the list.

Initial Messages

At the same time as setting up your list, you should also prepare your first postings to have them ready for launching the list. These include:

✓ Message to each person in the group to let them know when the list will be ready and telling them how to subscribe

✓ Welcome: introduce the list and its purpose

✓ Sign-In: invite everyone to introduce themselves

✓ How to Use the List: post initial instructions and ground rules

✓ Discussion Starters: postings intended to get the group started talking to each other, to be determined by the needs of your group

Also: Make sure you have your mailing list "info" file completed and installed. The sample "info" file above collects bits and pieces of all of the initial messages, which you can re-use and/or modify to post to the list.

You should now be ready to launch your list! Refer to the following Checklist to make sure you have all the pieces in place.

Archiving

For mailing lists to be an effective group collaboration tool, it's best to set up an archive of the discussion so the group can have a centrally accessible record of postings. Most list software comes with a built-in archiving function, but not a user-friendly one. For example, Majordomo keeps "log" files of each month's postings that subscribers can retrieve by emailing a request to the list server. If your list is an active one, this log file can be huge, and difficult to sort through. Check with your service provider to see which mailing list archiving tools they offer. Some networks offer WWW archive tools. This means every posting to the list gets copied to a WWW site for long-term storage. You can make the site accessible to just your group, or the general public. There is often a charge for this service, but it's well worth it in terms of the long-term usefulness of your online collaboration. Important: Make sure the service provider synchronizes archiving with the launch of your list.

All of these servers perform basically the same functions. We list several because webmail servers are a free service generously offered to the public. Depending on demand, some may come and go, so you may need to try a few before you get one that works. It's also best to choose the server that is closest to where you are located, to reduce Internet data congestion.

Web-to-Email Servers

Even though you're working together in email, you'll find a lot of use for **www** sites — especially for archiving your list and for reference to information relevant to your group. What do you do if people in your group don't have **www** access? An alternative method is to use email to retrieve the information from a **www** site by employing an online tool called a *webmail server.* By sending email to the addresses below, you can retrieve documents from almost any **www** site. For more information on webmail servers visit http://www.bellanet.org/email.html, or to receive a copy of an excellent guide to webmail servers send email to:

mail-server@rtfm.mit.edu

and enter only the following in the BODY of your message:

send usenet/news.answers/internet-services/access-via-email

The following is a list of current (June 1997) webmail servers, and links to documents on how to use these servers to access information.

WEBMAIL SERVERS (one can use any of these)

Send email to:	In the body of your message type ONLY the following:
getweb@unganisha.idrc.ca	GET http://... (then the URL)
getweb@info.lanic.utexas.edu	GET http://... (then the URL)
getweb@usa.healthnet.org	GET http://... (then the URL)
agora@dna.affrc.go.jp	send http://... (then the URL)
agora@www.eng.dmu.ac.uk	send http://... (then the URL)
agora@kamakura.mss.co.jp	send http://... (then the URL)
agora@mx.nsu.nsk.su	send http://... (then the URL)
w3mail@gmd.de	GET http://... (then the URL)
webmail@www.ucc.ie	GET http://... (then the URL)
web-mail@ebay.com	http://... (then the URL)

CHECKLIST

Use this checklist as a reference as you prepare to launch your mailing list. It brings together everything you need to do, from start to finish, to get your list up and running.

Mailing List Quick Reference

1 Contact the people you'd like to bring together online (by email where possible, otherwise by phone) to see if they are interested in working together using a mailing list, and what they'd need to enable them to do so. Also, identify those people who will help you do some of the planning. *(See: Planning Your List)*

2 Once you've done some list planning, do an initial check-in (by email where possible, otherwise by phone) with the people who will be participating on your list to tell them about the list, its purpose and when it will be launched, and find out if there's anything they need to be able to join in. Request a response from everyone you email so you can be sure they're receiving your messages. *(See: Planning Your List)*

3 If there are people you'd like to see participating who don't already have email accounts and/or the necessary equipment, see what you can do to help them get started. You may be able to find local support people to offer on-site setup and training.

4 After determining with your group how you would like the list to function, contact an Internet Service Provider to get it set up. *(See: Setting Up Your List)*

5 Get the first messages for the list ready, and prepare and install your mailing list "info" file. *(See: Setting Up Your List)*

6 *Test your list (and the archiving function if you've set one up) to see that it's working properly before announcing that it's open.* To do this, subscribe yourself, then make a test posting to see what happens. It's better to work out any technical problems *before* they can affect the whole group.

22

7 Launch the list. Send subscription instructions to all participants. Remind people to subscribe right away so that they don't miss any of the initial postings. (You can also subscribe everyone in the group yourself, but be sure that they are comfortable with this before you do it.)

8 Post initial topics (see 5. above), and invite responses.

9 Start a routine of checking in daily to see what's happening on the list (Online Facilitation). Welcome new participants as they introduce themselves.

10 Follow up with people who haven't subscribed and/or signed in to see if they need help.

11 If yours is a list where the general public is welcome, do some online promotion of your discussion area in other related online spaces. Be sure to include access instructions in your posting.

There is no set schedule for these steps. The pace of each group varies depending on the number of people involved and their readiness to use a mailing list. There may also be unanticipated delays at your Internet service provider. What's most important is that you take sufficient time to complete each step.

Part II

WORKING TOGETHER

ONLINE FACILITATION

What is Online Facilitation?

Facilitation online means paying attention to the social processes of the people you're working with electronically to enable the group to achieve its goals. The facilitator is the person or team that provides leadership in the group to get things going and keep them going. Just as in face-to-face facilitation, online facilitation can involve:

- helping your group articulate its goals
- creating a forum for discussion
- enabling broad participation
- promoting constructive debate
- when possible, moving shared ideas into action
- when not possible, acknowledging differences without debilitating the group
- working through specific activities (e.g., meetings, document development, information sharing, etc.)
- and the many other responsibilities which engage your skills with people, with group dynamics, and with mobilization.

An online facilitator deals with an added dimension — the unique qualities of mailing lists. Key among these are:

Transparency: From the moment it is launched, your mailing list is a written record of how your group works, what it accomplishes, how decisions are made and who is doing what.

Asynchrony: Group members will be online in different places and at different times. Expectations regarding pacing of communication and interaction need to be developed.

Text-Only Communication: Working together in type alone requires more care with each contribution, as well as skillful and unhurried interpretation.

Originally, when mailing lists first emerged, the role of the facilitator was limited to assuming technical responsibility for the orderly operating of the list: watching for

and dealing with error messages, and making sure people could access the discussion area, for example. More recently, understanding how people relate to one another and work together in an electronic workspace has become the primary function of the online facilitator.

Facilitation Roles

Good online facilitators are sensitive to the unique qualities of online workspaces, and how these can be applied to a group's particular collaboration needs. The online facilitator must first and foremost be a "people" person — technical know-how isn't mandatory and often gets in the way if not applied appropriately and sparingly. Here is what facilitators typically do:

- encourage and gently guide discussion
- make sure everyone gets to know each other
- plant ideas or start new topics of discussion
- help participants 'listen' to each other's postings
- bring together diverse threads of discussion into a summary
- periodically clarify the purposes of the list
- track down people that seem to be missing from the discussion
- be available to answer participants' questions
- keep discussion on track when a focused group interaction is taking place, such as an online meeting
- demonstrate good online form, with respect to formatting, quoting style, etiquette, etc. and gently point out when someone has made a mistake
- periodically circulate the group's "ground rules" to remind both veterans and newcomers how to work together
- help new users make the transition from private one-on-one email to list participation
- manage access permissions to the list
- mediate conflict.

Managing discussion and information-sharing on a mailing list is quite different from doing it in person. You don't have the same tools at your disposal as you do in a face-to-face meeting, such as a finite agenda or timekeeper. How much control you exert online really depends on the nature of what you're trying to achieve. If you are using your list to hold online meetings, you'll need to facilitate more actively than if the purpose of your list is general, less time-sensitive information-sharing and collaboration. Your first priority should be to help everyone achieve an online comfort level. That may mean giving up rigorous adherence to rules of how, where and what gets posted. The last thing you want to do is scare off a new participant by telling them they've posted something incorrectly.

Co-Facilitation

As you can see, there is a variety of work involved in facilitating your list. Depending on the size and volume of activity on your list, it's a good idea to identify people willing to share the work with you. Having someone watch the list and keep it moving at times when you're unavailable is important. If yours is a fairly active list, you may also want to identify people to focus on different areas: one person can concentrate on developing topic content, while another person concentrates more on the group process dynamics, for example. Co-facilitation is like co-leading a group of any kind. People sharing this responsibility need to be in touch regularly, and be clear about the division of work and the roles they are most effective at assuming. If you disagree on how a situation should have been handled, resolve your differences privately.

Occupational Hazards

Facilitation is emerging as a new online "job". It is an area where one can experiment and try new ways of doing things. There are some side effects to be aware of: you may feel exposed, lonely or unsupported at times. Working online means working in a very open manner and therefore you may be vulnerable to criticism in ways that are rarely available in other work environments. Public scrutiny of your work can take getting used to. If you are just starting out as a facilitator, be aware of this need for support.

You should seek support from other list facilitators and from your colleagues, to ensure you have a place to talk about what is happening (or not happening) on your list. Being able to ask questions regularly will keep you from getting stuck or frustrated. Using a co-facilitation approach can be a useful way to deal with this. Matching a new facilitator with a mentor who keeps an eye on the list, but posts to it only rarely, is another very effective way to reduce feelings of isolation. Finding a mentor is easier than you might think. Look around online, find a group you admire and ask them how they do it. If their facilitator is too busy they will probably know of others to recommend. Occasionally, an ISP will have a list for listowners and this can be a good forum for sharing list facilitation issues. If your ISP doesn't have one, you may want to suggest the idea to them.

Maintaining a List

The facilitator has a number of jobs to do, most of which can be handled in about fifteen minutes a day. The amount of time you actually spend depends on the other roles you have in the group you are facilitating. If you're also the project coordinator or a meeting chairperson, for example, you will spend longer on the list because that is where you do a lot of your work.

There are some things the facilitator needs to check every day, others that only need attention on an as-needed basis. Following are some guidelines for setting up your facilitation routine.

Facilitator — Daily

Attending to your list every day is critical. Not only does this allow you to keep things running smoothly, it signals your presence to the group and helps participants feel comfortable to express themselves.

Things you should scan for are:

✓ new people: welcome them

✓ requests for help or information: if there's been no answer from others, see if there's anything you can do, and post a note to let everyone know you're following up

✓ postings that you can help further develop to get people responding

Keep an eye out for problem postings:

✓ garbled postings: anything that looks to be in machine language or is completely indecipherable (e.g., file attachments) should be acknowledged as such — be sure to contact the person who posted it to let them know what the problem was and help them to re-post it

✓ brewing or outright conflict

✓ copyrighted material: it shouldn't be posted without permission from the author

To keep your list interesting and relevant you should also:

✓ be on the lookout for information and resources to share with the group

✓ be a bridge between your mailing list and any offline places your group works together.

Of course, you're not just the facilitator you're also a participant in the workspace so take the time you need to add your comments and start new topics of discussion.

Listowner — Daily

If you are also the listowner, you will have messages to watch for on a daily basis. The types of messages and responses to them depend on which mailing list software you are using. Here are some examples:

Subscription/Unsubscription messages: If your list is set up as "restricted" or "closed", you'll need to approve each subscriber. When your list is first launched, you will likely have many of these to deal with, so checking a few times a day to process them is a good idea, if it's feasible. Also, when people unsubscribe themselves from your list, you may get a confirmation message.

Bounced messages: Sometimes postings don't make it to the list, they are intercepted by the mailing list software and returned to the listowner. Some reasons for this are:

✓ the message author included a "trigger" word that the mailing list software thinks should be handled by the listowner (e.g., subscription, subscribe, help, etc.) rather than seen by the whole list of subscribers

✓ someone who hasn't been approved to access the list tries to post a message to it.

The listowner should keep a copy of the error messages on hand to learn their meanings, and until they have dealt with them. Generally, listowners are expected to deal with error messages within 24 hours.

Beware of Vacation Messages

Some people on your list may set up an automatic vacation message that responds for them when they are away. These can wreak havoc with your list, depending on how they are set up. You should advise people to unsubscribe or postpone receiving messages if they are going to be away. Often people will forget to do this, so as a backup you should also have them check that the settings on their vacation message are set as follows:

✓ make sure that their software DOES NOT quote the original incoming message in the vacation response (quoting can cause the same message to be repeated dozens or even hundreds of times to all list subscribers)

✓ the vacation program should be set to 'reply-to-sender' rather than 'reply-to-all'. This prevents the vacation message from going to all list subscribers.

In the event of a vacation message problem, you can unsubscribe them from the list. If feasible, leave a message for them by phone to let them know you've done this.

Weekly

If it's not happening naturally from within the group — and it may not for the first several weeks, ensure that there is at least one new posting a week, to keep people coming back to the list.

Periodically

The timing of these tasks depends on the volume of activity on your list. If yours is a very active list, you may need to attend to these tasks every month or so, or even more frequently. Also, See "Keeping Your List Active" for more ideas on ongoing facilitation work.

Look for Lost People

Sometimes people just disappear from the list. Perhaps their computer is malfunctioning, or they've been ill, or on vacation. Or it may be that the group work hasn't engaged them, or perhaps they don't feel comfortable there anymore. You should investigate to see if there's anything you or the group can do. If you find out that they will be offline for a while for some reason, post a note to the list to let everyone know.

Update Your "info" File

As your group defines the list and ways of working together, you should check to see that your "info" file reflects this evolution. You can replace the "info" file as often as you want. Even if there is no need to change it, you should circulate it from time to time to remind everyone why you're using the list and your accepted ways of collaborating.

Launch Anxiety

The first few weeks of a new list can be nerve-wracking. If you find the initial silence deafening, make sure you regularly (every few days) post something that will incite discussion. For example, post your own introduction and request that others do the same. Then you can post some of your initial ideas about what the group can accomplish in the space and ask for feedback. If you are expecting a particular group of people and some are missing, don't hesitate to contact them directly to see if they need assistance getting started. It's during the first few weeks that you'll be glad you did some initial thinking and strategizing about how to make effective use of your online workspace. It will pay off with quicker participation by your group members.

GUIDELINES FOR WORKING TOGETHER

Creating a comfortable and productive online environment with your group is your primary task as facilitator. Here are some strategies for making your list a friendly place:

Emphasize Good Manners

First and foremost, it's important that your group members treat each other respectfully. People tend to write online messages quickly, which can lead to misinterpretation and miscommunication. Remind your group to take extra care and be polite when posting. Similarly, when reading postings, members should try not to jump to negative conclusions. Clarifying questions, from either the facilitator or the group, are useful for sorting out any confusion. Over time your group will learn how each person communicates and how to work together.

Create A Safe Environment

People need to feel comfortable to express themselves to a group online. A person's sense of online safety comes from knowing how the list is supposed to work, what is expected of them as a member of that list, and how they should treat others. Establishing ground rules for the list with your group and intervening if people aren't working together respectfully are two ways to achieve this. A participant feels safe if they know that they can post their messages without fear of reprisal, and that they have someone (the facilitator) to turn to with problems or concerns.

Use Ground Rules

Over time, each mailing list takes on a personality of its own based on the people who are working together in it. To start, you should develop some basic guidelines with your group about how to cooperate on the list, and circulate them. Here are some standard topics that are usually covered:

✓ **Purpose of the list**: Outline why the list was set up and the topics to be addressed.

✓ **Participant expectations**: Ask newcomers to sign in. Indicate to them what the group expects with regard to regular monitoring and contributing.

From Workplace to Workspace

✓ **Cooperation**: Define the group code of conduct and how to handle conflict.

✓ **Where to get help**: Provide the facilitator's contact information so participants have someone to go to in the event of problems.

Take a look at the sample "info" file in *Setting Up Your List* for more ideas.

Make Sure People are "Listening" to Each Other

For some people, electronic messaging is a new form of communication, and they aren't attuned to its capacity to accommodate dialogue. Sometimes people get caught up in a flurry of posting messages and responding hastily to every item. Misinterpretation and conflict can arise when people neglect to take the time to look holistically at what the group is working on. As facilitator, it is important for you to focus list members when they appear not to be listening to one another.

Read Between the Lines

It may take some time to develop a sense of who the different people on your list are and how comfortable they feel, especially if you do not have the opportunity to meet them face-to-face. Drawing out the human tone and feelings from online text can be tricky. Never make assumptions about what you are reading. Always check with the original author if you are unsure. If you think others are also having a hard time interpreting a posting you can ask for clarification publicly on the list. Or, you can use private email to ask these questions and have the author make the clarification.

Assist Those Who Are Not Good Online Communicators

You will experience a wide variety of communicators on any mailing list. Some people communicate in text just as they talk, using punctuation and "smileys" to show emotion or expression of feelings. (*Smileys* are text-only happy faces :-) viewed sideways.) Others come across very formally online. The majority fall somewhere in between. Effective online communication is usually short and to the point, relevant to the topic underway, builds on the information already available, and is respectful in its

language and tone. It should also tell people what kind of feedback is needed, if a response is expected. To assist those who are poor online communicators you can model in your own postings how your group should post topics and responses.

Encourage individuals to exchange email with you as a way to develop confidence in posting. Many people are more comfortable using private email than posting to a mailing list, especially if they are new to online collaboration. Another strategy is to have the person post to you first for review: you can point out the parts of the posting that others might find difficult and ask them to rewrite the message. You can also use the *Posting Guidelines* in the Resources section to help your group communicate effectively.

Interpret the Silence

One of the first things people report when they begin posting to a list is the frustration they feel when no one responds to their messages. People are sometimes hesitant to respond to things unless they have something substantive to say. If someone agrees with the gist of a posting, they may not respond because they feel a posting containing only "Good idea!" is a waste of everyone's time. Instead, they'll wait till they have new insight or information to offer. Sometimes people are silent because they are unsure what the message means and don't want to look silly asking a clarifying question. Or, it may be that the person posting the message hasn't been clear about the kind of response they are looking for. As facilitator you can fill the silence with your own interpretations of why you think people are not responding or with seed postings to keep things rolling along. In some cases, groups establish a practice that if everyone remains silent on a suggestion it is generally accepted.

Include New People

As with any group of people, some will know each other better than others and some will feel more confident to jump right into the discussion than others. As new people join a list that has been running for some time your role as facilitator is like that of host at a gathering. Each new member should be encouraged to introduce themselves and relate their introduction to the focus of the work underway. Watch the postings from these new participants. They may need help with online etiquette or they may just feel like outsiders. Check in with them by private email to ensure they are feeling up to speed on what is happening, what is expected and how to post.

Help People Post

Newcomers to mailing lists may not be familiar with the convention of posting text-only, very plain messages. Unless your list is specifically set up to handle attachments, warn your group not to send them. You may need to do a bit of private coaching when problem messages get posted to the list. If the problem message is an attachment, try to get a text version posted that everyone can use. One of the fortunate things about attachments is that they are often large, so they may bounce to the listowner because they surpass the individual message size limit, so this can prevent them from even reaching the list. If someone posts very badly formatted messages, you can explain to them in private email the problems they are causing and how to use plain fonts (e.g., Courier 10), and wide margins so that their messages are easy to read.

Mediate Online Conflict

Using and reinforcing your group's collaboration and posting rules will go a long way to setting a respectful tone on the list. However, you should be prepared for the occasional flare-up between participants. Handling these situations carefully is something that you will learn to do over time. If you detect anger or attack online, always start by dealing with the individuals involved in private email, unless things have escalated to a point where you are concerned for the group as a whole. Most importantly, move slowly. Keep your messages short and to the point, and respond with a cool tone. As facilitator, your role is to address the workspace behaviour, not to engage in a debate of the issue that has caused the problem. Avoid lengthy or defensive responses. These situations are rare and are much more likely to happen in large public spaces than in smaller private or semi-private spaces.

KEEPING YOUR LIST ACTIVE

Mailing lists often start with a flurry of activity and then slow down over time. Each group establishes its own pace of working together online. Here are some ways to keep your list interesting after the initial excitement fades:

Share Information and Resources

Encourage all participants to act as pipelines to outside information sources. Your list is the one place everyone in your group has access to, but each member also brings their own individual interests and knowledge. Encouraging each member to post relevant resources they find online or offline creates a steady stream of new things for people to use in their work together.

Draw People In

Get your group participating by posting new topics and including suggestions about how they can respond. One way to invite response is to give people a deadline to post by. Another way is to end the posting with a question and exact instructions for how to respond. Using private email to reinforce the use of the list can also be helpful. Watch to see who is responding to messages and who is not. Supporting those who are by sending a quick email message with a comment about their contribution can be very encouraging. You can also send email to those who are not posting to ask them if they are having problems or are reluctant to post for some other reason.

Develop New Discussions

Just like you used seed topics to get things going in your workspace, you can also use them to maintain interest. For example:

- forward relevant items to the list, with your analysis and some questions included, or;

- start a topic requesting something from everyone, such as resources they have found useful.

Summarize and Synthesize Postings

A good facilitator will do online what they do in a meeting or workshop: summarize and synthesize what people are saying to keep the discussion moving and focused. Regularly capturing discussion to date, and then posting prompting questions to take the discussion to the next stage is a good way to maintain participation.

An excellent way to engage newcomers as well as reinvigorate veteran subscribers is to produce regular summaries. These outline what has transpired on the list over a period of time: background context (why the list exists), discussion highlights, decisions made, questions raised that still need answering, actions to be taken, next steps, resources identified, check-in on task delegation, etc. Summaries can also contain reminder information for everyone: how to access older postings, what the list is for, etc. Circulate parts or all of your summaries to other online venues, to keep them up to date on what you're doing, especially if your group has a number of workspaces with different groupings of participants.

Need a New List?

How will you know when you need to set up a new list? You will notice people complaining about too many postings which seem off-topic and yet important to some members of your group. Or, you may realize you have certain issues to which only some group members need access. Or, within your group there may be distinct geographic concerns and it would be useful to cluster people from the same region on a separate list. Sometimes, groups want a space that acts as a library for their documents, separate from any discussion or debate. In all cases, adding a new list can be accomplished quickly.

Some of your lists may be active longer than others, depending on their purpose. A list for planning an event will have a fixed time horizon, for example. It's good to keep dormant list archives around (if it isn't costing you a lot of money), as they provide a useful record of your group's work, and a reference point for newcomers. Before getting rid of them altogether, you can mine your old list archives for useful tidbits and post them in your active lists for reference.

If your group is using more than one list, establish mechanisms for sharing information between them, so people can keep tabs on what's going on without having to actively participate in several lists. Someone on each list can take responsibility for posting periodic summaries to the other lists, for example.

STEP-BY-STEP GUIDE TO SPECIFIC ACTIVITIES

You can use your mailing list for all sorts of work:

✓ sharing announcements about events

✓ asking questions and getting feedback from each other on your work

✓ posting reports and updates from programs and activities

✓ sharing newsletters and other resource materials for each other to borrow and build on

✓ pointing each other to relevant resources, online or offline

✓ planning logistics and content of meetings and other gatherings

✓ posting outcomes of meetings

✓ developing fundraising and/or advocacy campaigns

✓ developing position "papers"

✓ meeting new colleagues

Many people are now learning that mailing lists can also be used creatively for more complex and sustained, interactive group work. Facilitation is essential for these applications. Here are step-by-step approaches to carrying out specific group activities online:

PRODUCING DOCUMENTS TOGETHER
HOLDING MEETINGS ONLINE
PLANNING A FACE-TO-FACE CONFERENCE
DISSEMINATING RESEARCH MATERIAL

Producing Documents Together

You can use your mailing list to produce documents together: policy statements, position papers, funding proposals, reports, press releases, submissions to publications or conferences, newsletters, promotional materials, and more. The key steps are to outline the work, delegate responsibility for each piece, check on progress, and pull the pieces together for everyone to see. Be clear with the group about what they're expected to do throughout the process so that they can participate effectively. You'll also need the group to commit to providing timely feedback. As facilitator, your role is to get everyone working together and to keep the process moving forward. Here's how:

1. Present the project and timeline

Introduce the scope of the writing project and all the relevant details: context, deadline, audience, goals, size, etc.

2. Brainstorm content ideas and identify existing resources

Ask the group to suggest ideas for document content, and relevant work that already exists that can be drawn upon. You'll get an idea about who is interested in doing different sections by the responses. People will likely also start to discuss priorities for what they think should be included and what isn't necessary.

3. Draft a first outline and collect feedback

Identify someone to take the results of step 2 and pull together an outline of the document, indicating the deadline for feedback.

4. Post final draft outline

Feedback from step 3 should be incorporated into a final outline which is then re-posted to the group.

5. Delegate sections

Individuals should take responsibility for each section in the outline. Who and how many are involved depends on the specific task, people's workloads at the time, and the group's work habits. In some cases it makes sense for

one person to do the bulk of the writing, circulating sections to the group for feedback. In others, a more efficient approach is to have everyone do a section, with one person pulling the whole thing together. Using the list to develop the document means that even those people who can't be directly involved in the hands-on work, can still see the document's evolution as drafts get posted.

6. Post draft sections for feedback

As each section is finished, it should be posted to the group for feedback. The poster should be clear about the type of feedback needed (e.g., content, technical accuracy, style, etc.) and when it's needed by.

7. Pull the full document together

Once all of the sections have been posted, and have been checked over by the group, the full document can be pulled together and edited (by cutting and pasting the individual pieces into a single word-processed document). The full first draft should then be posted to the group for any additional feedback.

8. Edit/proofread

Steps 6 and 7 may be repeated a number of times until the document is ready for a final proofread.

9. Layout

Once the final text is assembled, it should be formatted for final production. You may only need a text version of the document, but it should still be arranged carefully for easy online reading. If you are doing a more complex non-text-only layout, be sure to also keep a text-only version of the final document for quick online reference.

10. Post final version

For the group's future reference, the final document should be posted to the list with a unique subject line, in both text-only and final formatted versions. This makes it easy for people to find and use again.

Production Tips

- It's easiest for everyone if all the draft writing is done in text-only format until it's ready for final production and formatting. This way people don't have to worry about accommodating different word processing programs, and everyone is able to see the document as it develops right on the list, without having to deal with file attachments.

- If some people are working on the same section, it's important for them to keep in close contact to avoid making changes to the same parts at the same time. You'll need to develop a system of "checking out" the sections being revised, and checking them back in again when ready for more feedback. When they are "checked out" no-one else can work directly on the text, but they can still send suggestions to the person who has checked them out.

- Some people may feel intimidated by posting draft work to the group. Before you start, be sure to warn the contributors not to take any editorial changes personally. Ask group members to use discretion when posting critical comments.

Holding Meetings Online

Facilitation is critical to successful online meetings, as is commitment from those "attending" to participate. There are also a number of steps to follow, which we have divided into two parts: things you need to do before the meeting starts, and those you do while the meeting is running.

Pre-Meeting Preparation

1. Set up a meeting space

It's best to set up a separate list for meetings only, so you can focus exclusively on the meeting agenda and keep all the relevant information in one place.

2. Set dates

Schedule a time for the meeting with the group. The amount of time needed depends on the complexity of the agenda topics and the number of people participating.

You need enough time for participants to be able to sufficiently digest and respond to the discussion. One to two weeks is a reasonable time frame — any longer and you'll lose momentum; any shorter and participants will feel rushed. Note: You'll need to leave extra time for non-Internet connected networks to receive and send messages. Often there are delays when working with networks in the South.

3. Identify a facilitator/chairperson

Attentive facilitation and chairing is critical to successful online meetings. You can rotate the facilitator role with each meeting, identify a particular facilitator just for meet ings or use the same person(s) you use for all your online facilitation. You may also identify people to chair particular topics within the agenda.

Meeting facilitation responsibilities include:

- Creating a framework for discussion and establishing a clear agenda. There are some standard topics that you'll always use, e.g., sign-in, updates, announcements and summaries, for example.

- Working with the group to establish and use online decision-making mechanisms

- Advising participants of expectations

- Advancing the discussion by raising key questions, summarizing, and identifying themes as they emerge

- Ensuring active participation by all: encouraging newcomers or "lurkers", and handling strong personalities who may dominate or disrupt the discussion for other participants

- Prompting participants by email to make sure they have an opportunity for input on all discussion topics

- Summarizing and closing the online discussion(s) by stating emerging consensus or calling a vote, if necessary.

4. Set the agenda

Participants need to know what the meeting priorities are in advance of the actual meeting. With the input of the group, the facilitator should draft and circulate the meeting agenda. The final version of the agenda should be posted at the start of the meeting, for reference.

5. Determine decision-making procedures

The group needs to agree on a way to make decisions online. For example, some groups will finish a discussion, summarize it and then hold a vote where silence signals agreement with the majority. You'll need to find a method that best suits the operating principles of your group. Sometimes the group won't be able to conclude discussion on a topic. These items can be moved forward to the next meeting, pending more information, or tabled till the next face-to-face meeting for more in-depth handling.

6. Send reminder and expectations

As the start date of the meeting gets closer, circulate a reminder message to all participants by email. You should also remind people of their meeting responsibilities: sign-in, daily check-in, posting reports, participating in discussion, voting, etc.

Running the Meeting

7. Open the meeting

The facilitator should post a "Start of Meeting" topic that includes a request for sign-in.

It's important to get as many people to the meeting as quickly as possible, so you can maximize the use of the time you have together. Track down anyone who hasn't signed in within a couple of days.

8. Post initial topics

Post the initial topics at the start of the meeting, e.g., Financial Report, Announcements, Member Updates, etc., as well as clearly labeled topics that correspond to each item in the agenda. The facilitator, or the chair of each issue, can also open the discussion on each of these items.

9. Synthesize discussion

To help everyone work through the agenda, the facilitator should periodically synthesize discussion on each topic and present the options that have emerged, for further discussion or for decision.

10. Do a half-time check-in

Midway through the meeting, summarize the work completed to that point, and indicate any items still to be addressed. This will focus participants on the meeting priorities. It's also a good opportunity to remind everyone how much time is left in the meeting, and to encourage participation.

11. Encourage participation

Prompt people (especially those who aren't actively participating) by email throughout the meeting to ensure discussion on all topics is advanced.

12. Start to wrap up

Notify everyone that the meeting will soon be coming to a close, and highlight items still needing attention. At this point you can check in to see if the group wants to extend the meeting time to address particular issues.

13. Close the meeting

On the specified date, declare the meeting closed. Present what will happen with unresolved items, e.g., if they're being postponed till the next meeting, being further developed by those interested in doing so, etc.

14. Post a meeting summary

After the meeting has ended, the facilitator should post a summary: final decisions, unresolved discussions, and any other important information. The summary serves as a condensed record of the meeting, as well as a way for participants to verify the decisions.

Here are some sample messages from an online meeting:

Introductory message:

```
** Topic: START OF SEPTEMBER 1997 MEETING **

This marks the start of the September 1997 online
meeting.

Please sign in and let us all know you're here.

The meeting is scheduled to go to September 18. Please
follow this meeting closely these next 2 weeks as we want
to make sure it is thoroughly completed.
```

Just so people remember, the policy for online meetings
is that all board members are expected to participate. If
for some reason someone cannot participate, please
designate another person from your organization to
participate and vote in your place.

Other staff are welcome to follow the meeting, and to
post information if needed.

Here is a sample meeting agenda. Note how the facilitator has indicated the action items each participant needs to take:

-- Agenda - September 1997 Online Meeting --

TO DO

All members complete new Member Report Form and reply to
     "Member REPORTS - September 1997" topic.

Look over Management Systems topics and post any edits.

Anyone who has reports, please post them:
     Executive Board on activities to date.
     Women's Programme, Fatima
     Africa Programme, Charles
     WWW/Intranet team, Sally
     Fundraising, Rhona
     Lobbying, Roberto
     Outreach, Pat
and any others as needed.

DISCUSSIONS

The consultant's letter of Challenges and Solutions based
on the strategic planning report. See the
"Challenges/Solutions: New Structure" topic.
**   This is a particularly important topic to read
carefully and respond to.**

Dates for 1998 Board Meeting in Mexico. In "1998 Council
Meeting, dates" topic.

Possible opportunity for free services from a corporate
sponsor in "Corporate Sponsor" topic.

WWW Development proposal to analyze in
     "WWW Development proposal" topic.

How to address problems that some members are having in
     "Members in Trouble and Transition" topic.

VOTE

(background information is posted for each vote topic)

Vote on new half-time position to hire in
     "PROPOSAL: Financial Manager" topic.

Vote on establishment of new program in
    "PROPOSAL: Human Rights Programme" topic.

Vote on new policy of multiculturalism in the
    "POLICY: Multilingualism" topic.

Planning a Face-To-Face Conference

A common and effective use of mailing lists is to plan face-to-face conferences. If the conference you are planning is fairly large, and public, you will probably need a few lists to meet all your needs.

For internal planning purposes, you can use your list to determine:

✓ conference agenda

✓ presentations/workshops/speakers

✓ logistics: date, location, accommodation, travel

✓ who to invite

If it is a public conference, you will also need to circulate information about the conference as well as conference proceedings and summaries to relevant public lists. You may want to set up a new list for public communication about the conference.

Here's an online planning overview:

1   The idea for the conference will need to originate somewhere, either from within the group or from an external process.

2   Announce the need for planning on the list, indicate the roles that need to be filled and estimated time commitments, and see who's interested in participating.

3   The planning group, once identified, can post draft outlines of each of the major conference components (agenda, logistics, etc.) for feedback. These postings should include deadlines for getting feedback from the group. For in-depth work on the various planning aspects of the conference, the planning group should set up their own working list from which they post finalized items to the full group.

4   Once the agenda and logistics planning are complete, information about the conference can be circulated to other lists, WWW sites, etc. so people can plan to attend.

5   While the conference is taking place, it's helpful to those not attending to be able to see the highlights from each day's work. You can set up a short-term list just for this purpose. Consider having someone post a daily summary.

6   When the meeting is completed, a final report or minutes can be posted to the public conference list.

Disseminating Research Material

As online facilitator of a group that produces research material, it is your job to get people in the habit of sharing their work, in a useful way.

First of all, you'll need to be familiar with the research undertakings of the group. Have each participant post an abstract of what they are working on and describe resources they have found useful in that work. Encourage group members to ask questions about each other's work, so you can learn more about the types of information that are useful to the group. You should also open a discussion amongst the researchers about what would be useful to them in a research archive: which information, how it should be organized, etc.

While your group can continue to use a general list for discussion, it's best to set up a separate moderated list for the sole purpose of collecting relevant findings and documents. The separate moderated list allows you to clearly label and organize the material for easy retrieval, as well as check it over for formatting and readability, before it gets posted. You should also make sure this list is set up with a user-friendly list archiving tool so that people can easily navigate through the postings. This way, they needn't subscribe to it, but can visit it as needed.

Once you have established the archive list, periodically check in with each researcher to see if they have anything ready to report. Indicate the specifications for formatting documents that are being sent to the archive, and have them email their findings to the archive list. You should post regular updates to the discussion list of new documents posted to the archive list.

Part III

RESOURCES

This guide provides an overview of the work involved in setting up and animating a mailing list. However, you will probably run into unique situations that haven't been addressed here. This section answers some typical facilitator questions, and provides pointers to additional sources of support.

Facilitator Q&A

1. *How do I delete postings?*

    You can't remove a posting once it's been posted. However, you can post a follow-up message with a correction or explanation.

2. *How often should I circulate the rules our group has developed?*

    How frequently you circulate the rules varies from group to group. If membership on your list changes regularly it's good to circulate them every few months, or when you've noticed several new people sign up. Also, if a problem arises that the rules address, you can re-post them to remind everyone of the group's code of conduct.

3. *One of our users always quotes the entire message they're responding to and adds their comment at the bottom. What do I do?*

    Email them privately explaining the inconvenience they are causing the rest of the members on the list, and show them how to quote selectively. Warn them that their comments may be missed if people can't easily find them. Include a sample of effective quoting, and invite them to practice responding with you a few times before going back to the list.

4. *Some people seem to be dominating the list, and others we rarely hear from. How can we achieve a better balance?*

    As in face-to-face facilitation, you need to make sure everyone's engaged in the discussion, and make space for those who aren't making themselves heard. Check in with those you aren't hearing from to find out why they aren't posting. Also, on the list, acknowledge those you've already heard from and request participation from others who have been quiet. It may also be time

to check in with the group to see if the list is meeting their needs. See if the original list purpose is still valid and/or if you need an additional list for separate discussions.

5. *Everyone seems to post to me directly, instead of to the list. It's doubling my workload. How can I get them to stop?*

    First of all, make sure that your list has been set up so that replies go to the list. You can check this yourself or ask the service provider. If the settings are correct, perhaps people aren't sure if their postings are relevant and they are writing to you to be on the safe side. Remind individuals that they can feel free to post directly to the list. You can also do a posting to the group reminding them of the purpose of the list and the issues that are relevant, to increase their comfort level.

6. *Our list has been running for six months, and someone new just joined. How do we bring them up to speed?*

    There are many ways to include newcomers that depend on how you've set up your list. As long as your "info" file is up to date, they should get a good overview of what the list is for and how they can participate. You can point them to any summaries you have done recently that provide highlights of the group's work. If your list has an archive, you can have them start there to skim through the past postings to get caught up. Be sure to welcome them on the list. Follow up by private email to see how they are doing.

7. *I run a list where information on the same topic will be coming from a variety of sources. How can I prevent duplicate messages that will annoy everyone?*

    Here are three possible solutions:

    1   Make the list moderated, so that every posting goes to the listowner who will ensure that only one copy of each report gets posted.

2   Make arrangements with your group so that different people on the list have exclusive responsibility for covering certain issues.

3   Set up two lists: one open to everyone for discussion, news, etc., and a separate moderated one just for reports.

8.   Can viruses be transmitted through mailing lists?

Yes they can, but there are precautions you can take to avoid this. The good news is you cannot get a virus from exchanging ascii (text-only) messages. However, you should make sure that each person uses current anti-virus software if you will be using your list to exchange file attachments.

Posting Guidelines

Here are some conventions and suggestions for posting messages that make it easier for everyone to work together on a mailing list:

Be brief

Limit your postings to one or two screens in length. Particularly in the South, many people must pay for the volume and number of messages they receive. Be considerate of this constraint and post pointers to sources of further information (e.g., yourself, URL, etc.).

Be readable

Make sure your text-only messages are easy to read: use blank lines to unclutter them, and format them as carefully as you would a more formal document.

Address messages correctly

Make sure you address your messages to the correct list address. Often, there are a number of addresses associated with a list: the listowner, the list itself, and the machine that runs the list. If you're replying to a message, this shouldn't be a problem as replies should go directly to the list.

Watch your language

If your list subscribers don't all speak the same language, avoid using slang or idioms, unless you're prepared to explain them. If your group is able to work in multiple languages, beware of accented characters. It's best to remove accents and post plain unaccented text unless you have confirmed that everyone's software can cope with them.

Give your postings clear titles

When you post a new message or a reply, check the subject line to ensure it reflects the content of the message. Label your topics clearly to give readers an idea of what to expect.

Use headings such as Event:, News:, Info:, Draft:, URGENT:, Summary:, etc., and provide some context. Limit yourself to 35 characters (including spaces) or less, to make your Subject line fully readable. For example, PROPOSAL: Global Women's Networking.

Text is easiest

Post your messages in plain text ONLY. Do not send file attachments unless your list is specifically set up to handle them. Regardless of hardware and software differences, everyone can read plain text online (also known as DOS text, ascii text and text only). If you need to share a non-text file (e.g., a formatted Word document, a spreadsheet, etc.), suggest that those who have the appropriate software to use the file request it directly from you via private email.

Give options

When citing additional resources, remember that some people in your group may not have full WWW access. Be sure to provide alternative ways to get the information. For example, you can provide the address of a Web-to-email gateway (see the Setting Up Your List section for more information). Or, you can offer to get the resource for them and email it to them.

Avoid fancy fonts

When using wordprocessor software, compose with a non-proportional (fixed) 10 pitch font like Courier, to avoid posting a messy message with full lines followed by line fragments (which happens when you use proportional fonts, like Times, etc.). When in doubt, send a test message to yourself first.

Identify yourself

Sign your messages with your name and email address. Some software fails to capture the sender's name from the header, making it impossible to follow up privately.

Use private email when appropriate

When you would like to have a personal discussion, or if you feel offended by a particular message, send a message to the individual involved only.

Quote selectively

Quoting someone's previously posted text is very helpful when done correctly:

- if there is a long "header" on the message (the information at the top of a message that shows how it traveled from system to system to reach its final destination), delete everything but the name/ID of the person you're quoting and the date and subject line of the message

- quote only the individual pieces you're responding to, and insert your responses right after the quotes to help everyone follow your logic

- only repeat enough text to help you build on the original point.

  IMPORTANT! Remove headers from messages in the body of the posting. Failing to delete To: lines in the body of messages can mean that your message is not posted. Mailing list software may reject such headers as a precaution against mail loops (the same message cycling continuously between two lists).

Indicate your tone

Sarcasm, irony, and humor can backfire online. "Smiley" symbols such as :-) and :-(viewed sideways are universally used to show smiles and frowns and, when added to the end of a sentence, indicate you aren't being too serious.

Create single-subject messages whenever possible

This makes it easier for people to respond to the original topic. If there are several issues raised in one posting, offshoot conversations will start up under the one topic making it harder to dig them out when you need to in the future.

Don't hesitate to start a new topic

If what you want to say doesn't fit into any of the existing topics, start a new one. If you're responding to an existing topic, but your response engenders a new thread of discussion, start a new topic and point people to the new one in your response to the old one. It's also good to separate out any documents (e.g., proposal, summary, strategy, etc.) that result from discussion as their own topics, so that they're easy to find, rather than burying them in the responses to the original topic.

Re-read your messages

Once a message is sent, it's gone forever. You can't get it back. And when you're sending it to a group it will be around for quite some time. Be sure to re-read your messages before you send them, particularly ones dealing with sensitive issues, to make sure the words you have typed are really communicating what you intend to say. It's easier to make changes before the message leaves your computer, than to make apologies or give explanations to a larger group after the fact.

Don't shout

Typing your messages in ALL CAPITAL LETTERS comes across as SHOUTING online. It's also hard on the eyes. Regular sentence case is the norm, although some people tend to the other extreme of all lower case, which seems generally acceptable also.

Warn before long messages

If you must post a long or large file, warn readers at the top of the message about the size and content, so they can skip it if they wish. Better yet, just tell people you have the file and those that are interested can email you for a copy. Access and downloading charges are particularly expensive in the South.

Forward selectively

When you forward to the list a message you've come across elsewhere, leave out the big, long header and just forward enough so that everyone can see the source of the posting. Also, include your own comments about why you're sharing the forwarded posting.

Ask before posting email

ALWAYS check with the original sender before copying a private email message to the list. They may have had a reason for posting to you privately that you aren't aware of.

Limit your cross-posting

If you see something relevant to the group elsewhere on-line, tell people what it is and where to find it, rather than re-posting the whole thing (unless it's really short). They may have already come across it in their online travels, and don't want to see the same stuff everywhere they go.

Develop tolerance for informality

Messages online tend towards informality. Many people choose to write in their own unique mix of upper and lower case characters, and use more free-form punctuation. You'll also notice a lot more spelling mistakes online than offline. Mistakes tend to be the rule rather than the exception as people often type their responses quickly, and are conscious of the time it's taking them. Avoid critiquing typos unless they occur in critical places, like addresses, phone numbers, URLs, etc.

Further Reading

The following references provide useful information on facilitating group work:

Anatomy of High Performing Teams: A Leaders Handbook, M. Laiken, 1994, OISE Press, Toronto, ON. To order a copy, send a message to: **utpbooks@utpress.utoronto.ca**

Working Together Online, Maureen James and Liz Rykert, 1997, Web Networks, Toronto, ON. See **http://community.web.net/wto** for more information.

The Skilled Facilitator — Practical Wisdom for Developing Effective Groups, Roger M. Schwarz, 1994, Jossey-Bass Inc, San Francisco, CA.

Collaborating — Finding Common Ground for Multiparty Problems, Barbara Gray, 1989, Jossey-Bass Inc, San Francisco, CA.

Managing Projects in Organizations — How to Make the Best Use of Time, Techniques, and People, J. Davidson Frame, 1988, Jossey-Bass Inc, San Francisco, CA.

For more information on the last three books, see **http://www.jbp.com** or email **webperson@jbp.com**

Also, you will find a good introduction to online group collaboration at:

http://www.oise.utoronto.ca/~arojo/forums.htm

About the Institution

The International Development Research Centre (IDRC) is a public corporation created by the Parliament of Canada in 1970 to support technical and policy research to help meet the needs of developing countries. The Centre is active in the fields of environment and natural resources, social sciences, health sciences, and information sciences and systems. Regional offices are located in Africa, Asia, Latin America, and the Middle East.

About the Publisher

IDRC Books publishes research results and scholarly studies on global and regional issues related to sustainable and equitable development. As a specialist in development literature, IDRC Books contributes to the body of knowledge on these issues to further the cause of global understanding and equity. IDRC publications are sold through its head office in Ottawa, Canada, as well as by IDRC's agents and distributors around the world.

About the Authors

Maureen James is an Internet communications and project consultant. Currently based in Johannesburg, South Africa, Ms James is coordinating a women's networking project at SANGONeT, a member network of the Association for Progressive Communications. Liz Rykert is an organizer and community development worker based in Toronto, Canada. Using tools from advocacy to online meetings, Ms Rykert assists groups to establish effective electronic strategies rooted in their daily work. Together, Maureen James and Liz Rykert recently coauthored the book *Working Together Online* (Web Networks, Toronto, Canada, 1997).